If I Were a Kid in Ancient Rome

Cricket Books

Peterborough, NH

Staff

Editorial Director: Lou Waryncia
Editor: Ken Sheldon
Book Design: David Nelson, www.dnelsondesign.com
Designer: Ann Dillon
Proofreader: Eileen Terrill

Text Credits

The content of this volume is derived from articles that first appeared in *AppleSeeds* and *Calliope* magazines. Contributing writers: Anne Austin, Joann Burch, Sabine Goerke-Shrode, Cyndy Hall, Anthony Hollingsworth, Kathiann M. Kowalski, Gloria W. Lannom, Patricia D. Lock, Kathleen M. Muldoon, Jane Sutcliffe.

Picture Credits

Photos.com: Cover, 4, 28; Photo-Objects.net: Cover; Shutterstock: Cover, 1, 4, 5 (both), 7 (both), 11, 12, 20, 23 (both); Clipart.com: 15 (top), 19, 20, 27; Werner Forman / Art Resource, NY: 15 (bottom); North Wind Picture Archives: 18–19.

Illustration Credits

Beth Stover: 3, 10–11, 23; Annette Cate: 6, 16–17; Tim Foley: 8–9, 12; Cheryl Jacobsen: 13; Chris Wold Dyrud: 14; Dave Edwards: 21, 22; Mark Mitchell: 24–25, 26–27.

Library of Congress Cataloging-in-Publication Data

If I were a kid in ancient Rome / Lou Waryncia, editorial director ; Ken Sheldon, editor. -- 1st ed.

    p. cm. — (Children of the ancient world)

    Includes index.

    ISBN-13: 978-0-8126-7930-4 (hardcover)

    ISBN-10: 0-8126-7930-X (hardcover)

    1. Children—Rome—Juvenile literature. 2. Rome—Civilization—Juvenile literature.
    3. Rome—Social life and customs—Juvenile literature.
    I. Waryncia, Lou. II. Sheldon, Kenneth M. III. Series.

    DG91.I35 2006

    937—dc22   2006014674

Cricket Books

a division of Carus Publishing

30 Grove Street, Suite C

Peterborough, NH 03458

www.cricketmag.com

Printed in China

Table of Contents

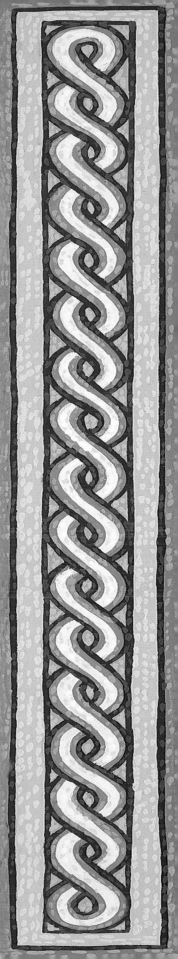

Gifts from the Romans

The Romans built aqueducts throughout their empire to carry water to the places where it was needed. This aqueduct in southern France has a water channel on the top level and a road on the lower level.

f you lived in ancient Rome, you would find many things that are similar to today. Here are a few of the things we can thank the Romans for.

Rub-a-dub-dub

When you take a shower or bath, you're enjoying the advances the Romans made in indoor plumbing. They pioneered the use of *aqueducts*, pipes and channels that brought water from rivers and lakes over long distances to the city. Romans bathed daily, and their public baths were the forerunners of our fitness clubs—complete with swimming pools and hot tubs!

A Capital Idea

The capital letters that we learn in school are almost the same as those the Romans took with them as they conquered the western world. Many of the words that Roman kids would have learned in school would look familiar, too. At least 70 percent of the English language comes from Latin, the Romans' language. Almost every English word with more than five letters can be traced back to the ancient Romans.

Measuring Up

If you go to the grocery store to buy a pound of hamburger, you're using Roman measurements. A Roman pound was called a *libra*, from which we get our abbreviation "lb" for pound. If you walk home a mile, that's Roman, too. The modern mile is based on the Roman *mille passus*, or "1000 paces," each pace being about 5 Roman *pedes* (feet). And one-twelfth of a Roman foot was an *uncia*, which is where our word "inch" comes from.

Milestones like the one above told Roman travelers how far they had to go. Julius Caesar, below, introduced the calendar upon which our modern calendar is based.

Year In and Year Out

The calendar we use is based on the Julian calendar, named after Julius Caesar. It was the first calendar to have a 365-day year with an extra day every fourth (or "leap") year. Many of our months are named after

Roman gods (January and March for Janus and Mars), Roman rulers (July and August for Julius Caesar and Caesar Augustus), or Roman numbers (September to December for the numbers 7 to 10—the Romans began their year in March).

The Original Mall

Did you know that the Romans constructed the first mall? It had covered halls and housed 150 shops and offices. The emperor Trajan had it built, and you can still see its ruins in Rome today.

Down the Road

To get to a mall, you need to get on a highway. The Romans perfected long-lasting roads by digging away the dirt, then putting down layers of rock, sand, and gravel. Finally, they surfaced it with paving stones or concrete. The top layer was called the *pavimentum*, from which we get our word "pavement."

Law and Order

Rome's greatest gift to us may be its legal code. The Romans saw rules and regulations as a way of giving people individual rights and protecting them from the state and from each other. Roman law has served as the foundation of legal codes in all western countries, including the United States. Even the way we create laws in the United States is similar to the way it was done in ancient Rome. When the Founding Fathers established our democratic way of government, they modeled it on the Roman Republic, which had two governing bodies that were responsible for making laws.

Justicia, the Roman goddess of justice, symbolized the Roman approach to law. She was often shown with scales representing fairness.

Guide to the Gods

Over the centuries, Romans worshipped many different gods and often adopted the gods of the lands they conquered. In fact, many of the major Roman gods were the same as Greek gods, but with different names.

Roman God	Dominion	Greek God
Jupiter	King of the gods	Zeus
Juno	Queen of the gods	Hera
Apollo	Sun, music, medicine	Apollo
Bacchus	Wine	Dionysus
Diana	The moon, hunting	Artemis
Mars	War	Ares
Mercury	Travel, commerce	Hermes
Minerva	Wisdom, the arts	Athena
Neptune	The sea	Poseidon
Pluto	The underworld	Hades
Venus	Love, beauty	Aphrodite

Neptune, Roman god of the sea, was borrowed from the Greek god Poseidon.

At Home in Rome

Rome was a crowded city, and people lived wherever they could find space. Romans lived above shops, in apartment buildings, or—if they were wealthy—in lovely houses with gardens. Some Romans also had *villas* (country estates).

Does it ever rain inside your house? It would if you lived in ancient Rome. Every house, or *domus*, had a large, square hole in its roof. The hole let in sunlight and fresh air, but it let the rain in, too. A pool below caught the rainwater.

The front of the house was for company. The most important room was a grand reception hall called an *atrium*, where the man of the house received important people who came to call.

The rear of the house was only for the family. Most of the family's time was spent in the enclosed garden courtyard. Bedrooms, bathrooms, the kitchen, and the dining room all opened onto the garden. The garden was their only view. For privacy, Roman houses had no windows facing the street.

VI. A walkway around the garden, supported by marble columns, provided shade in the hot Roman summers.

V. Bedrooms were tiny, with just room for a bed and perhaps a chair.

IV. The atrium was richly decorated with mosaics, statues, and fine wall paintings but not much furniture.

III. Each day the family prayed at this shrine to the household gods.

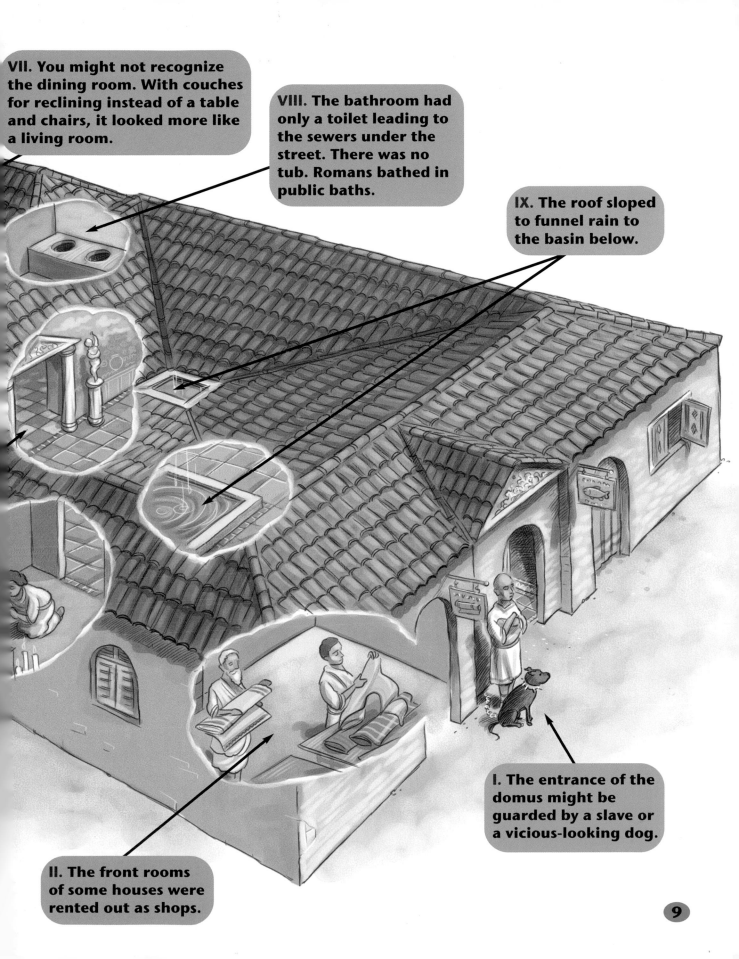

Bathing... with Friends?

At bathtime, you get into the tub, soap yourself, soak, rinse off, and you're done. Bathing was different in ancient Rome.

Although rich Romans had water piped into their houses, most people did not bathe at home. They went to government-run public baths called *thermae*. Two thousand years ago, there were almost a thousand public baths in Rome. These huge buildings were among the city's most important buildings.

Water was piped into the baths from outside the city. Also, rain fell through an opening in the roof, into a pool in the *atrium*, or open space. At the *thermae*, the water was heated by a furnace called the *praefurnium*.

Raised by Wolves?

According to legend, Rome was founded in 753 B.C. by twin brothers, Romulus and Remus, who were raised by a she-wolf. Rome fell in A.D. 476, under its last emperor, Romulus Augustulus.

Women usually visited the baths in the morning, and men went there in the afternoon. After undressing and storing their clothes in cabinets, bathers entered the *unctorium,* where their bodies were rubbed with olive oil— the Romans did not use soap. First, they exercised in the *gymnasium.* Then slaves removed the oil and dirt from their bodies with a metal scraper.

The bathers moved on to the *tepidarium,* a steam room with heated walls and floors. They wore thick-soled sandals to protect their feet from being burned. Still somewhat oily, they soaked in very hot water in the *caldarium.*

From there, they went to the *frigidarium* and plunged into a cold-water pool to close the pores of their skin. Finally, they returned to the *unctorium,* where

they were massaged, oiled, and perfumed.

The Romans did not go to the baths just to get clean. The baths were community meeting places. People chatted with friends, watched games, walked in the gardens, ate snacks sold by fast-food vendors, visited the shops, and read scrolls in the library. In a way, the public baths were the health clubs and recreation centers of ancient Rome.

With seating for twenty people, this public latrine in the Roman city of Ostia Antica was probably a popular place to meet your neighbors.

Public Potties

In ancient Rome, most people didn't have indoor plumbing, which meant no indoor bathrooms. Instead, they went to a public potty, or *forica*. The *forica* had marble benches with holes set at regular spaces around three sides of a room. Underneath the benches, a channel with constantly flowing water washed away wastewater into a sewer system. Users cleaned themselves with sponges, which they rinsed in the water running in a trough in front of them. Users paid a small fee for the privilege of using the *forica,* making it the first "pay toilet."

BRITAIN

Germania
(GERMANY)

Gaul
(FRANCE)

EUROPE

Hispania
(SPAIN AND
PORTUGAL)

ITALY

• Rome

GREECE

AFRICA

Mediterranean Sea

EGYPT

The World of Rome

Want to Play Latrunculi?

Kids in ancient Rome had lots of different toys, like hobby-horses, wooden soldiers, and spinning tops. Girls had dolls made of wax, rags, wood, ivory, and terra-cotta (baked clay). Some dolls even had movable arms and legs. (Our word "puppet" comes from the Latin word for doll, *pupa.*)

Archaeologists have found paintings of Roman children playing with kites, yo-yos, jump ropes, and swings. They also liked to play games like leapfrog, tag, and blindman's bluff. In a game called *rex* (Latin for "king"), a group of children would choose one person to be the king, who could then command the rest of them to perform whatever he asked.

Another popular game was called odd or even, where one player held stones or bones in his or her closed fist. The other player had to guess whether the number of objects was odd or even.

Romans played board games like *duodecim scripta* ("twelve lines"), which looked like our game of backgammon. Like the Greeks, they also had a board game similar to our checkers or chess, except they called it *latrunculi*, Latin for "little robbers."

Another game, which was especially popular among women, was *micare digitis*, Latin for "to move the fingers rapidly." Two players would raise their right hands and shout out how many fingers the other was about to extend. The person who five times correctly guessed the number of fingers her opponent extended was declared the winner.

Roman kids liked outdoor sports, too, including hunting, fishing, footraces, and even bowling. Young and old enjoyed hoop-rolling, rolling a metal hoop by hitting it with a stick. Sometimes, they attached small bells to the hoop to make a jingling noise as it rolled along.

Kids and adults also enjoyed swimming. They held contests to see who could swim farthest from the shore. Some wealthy people even had swimming pools, which might be heated or open-air pools filled with seawater.

When we toss a coin, we say, "Heads or tails?" Roman children called out, "Heads or ships?" Their coins had the face of the god named Janus on one side and a ship on the other.

On the night before her wedding day, a Roman girl would put her toys on the altar of her parents' household gods, like the one shown here. This meant she was grown up.

Monkeys & Magpies

Just like you, Roman children often had pets. Some were ordinary pets, like cats and dogs. Others were for ornament or entertainment.

Birds were popular pets. Hoots, chirps, and songs of caged birds filled many Roman homes. Some folks kept owls. Others listened to the chattering of magpies. People who loved music kept nightingales, which filled the air with their golden melodies.

Many Roman homes had special

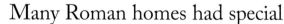

pigeon coops on their roofs. Pigeons served as mail carriers, delivering messages wired to their feet.

Some Romans kept pet fish in outdoor ponds. Turbot, which are flat, diamond-shaped fish, were common. Some turbot owners decorated their fish with necklaces and gold rings. Others were even buried with pictures of their turbot.

In their gardens, Romans often had more than just flowers. Many had pet monkeys, which loved to entertain their owners. They might also have pet goats or ponies for the children to hitch to wagons.

Romans kept small Maltese dogs as "lap dogs," and carried them everywhere, even to school. At night, the dogs slept in their masters' beds. Archaeologists have found dog collars and tags with the owners' names in case the dogs got lost.

Romans also loved cats, and not just as house pets. Cats worked to keep mice and rats out of the grain barrels. Roman soldiers were known to carry their cats into battle. Some people kept large wild cats, like lions, in their homes. But these definitely were not lap cats!

17

What's for Cena?

Imagine you've been invited to eat with a friend in ancient Rome. What's on the menu? Pizza? Spaghetti? No, those foods weren't invented until much later.

In the early days, the Romans ate simply, much like the Greeks, from whom they borrowed many of their ideas. Breakfast (or *jentaculum*) was usually bread seasoned with salt or honey and dipped in wine. If you were wealthy, you would lie on cushions set out in the courtyard of your villa, as slaves served heaping platters of wine-soaked bread, olives, cheese, and fruit such as dates or raisins.

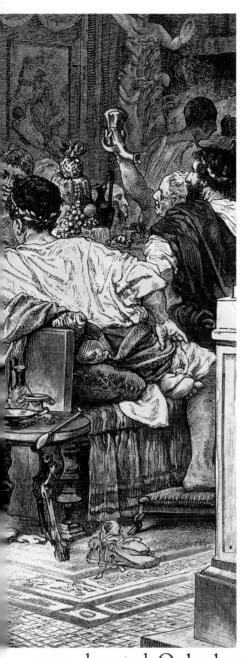

On the streets, workmen and schoolboys bought rolled-up pancakes or thick slices of dark bread at bakeries. Poor and unemployed Romans lined up on the street called *Via Sacra* (the "Sacred Way") to receive the government's daily distribution of free bread.

Romans would eat lunch (*prandium*) at home with their families, or at a friend's house. For the poor, this was usually more bread. The rich didn't eat much for lunch either: cheese, fruit, and bread dipped in wine. During lunch, the shops closed, students walked home for a two- or three-hour break from school, and the streets were deserted. Only slaves and the poorest Romans worked through the midday break.

Dinner (or *cena*) was the big meal of the day. Still, for ordinary people this meant more bread, along with beans, cabbage, or vegetable soup. If they were lucky, they had a little meat. Everything was cooked in one pot, and the whole family dug in with their fingers. Romans didn't eat with forks and spoons.

Like many people in the ancient world, the Romans ate while reclining on couches, rather than sitting on chairs, as we do. Wealthy men often threw elaborate dinner parties with several courses, much wine, and entertainment.

Hist-O-Bit

Bread was the main staple of the Roman diet. The typical loaf of bread was 2 inches thick, round, and cut into wedges like a pizza.

Wealthy merchants and nobles often hosted large dinner parties, but these were for men only. Dinner was served in three courses. First there were appetizers like olives, anchovies, vegetables, and herbs. Next came a meat dish, such as roasted baby goat, ostrich, venison, or sometimes salted fish. Then it was time for dessert, which was usually fresh fruit—grapes, figs, plums, or apples.

The rich ate with their fingers, too, but they used spoons to serve themselves and toothpicks to pick up food. Eating this way made their fingers sticky, so they had bowls of water on the table for washing their hands after each course. Often in wealthier households, musicians provided entertainment during a meal.

As the Romans conquered the world, they learned about new and more exotic dishes. Seeking new foods and dishes became an obsession for the wealthy. They ate things like peacock brains, flamingo tongues, and milk-fed snails. Maybe you're glad you weren't rich in ancient Rome!

Ancient Romans often stopped for a bite to eat or drink at a *thermopolium,* a kind of Roman fast-food restaurant. The jars set into the counter held hot foods and drinks, perfect for busy Romans on the go.

Reading & Writing the Roman Way

Ever wish you didn't have to go to school? In ancient Rome, only children from wealthy families went to school. Poorer children learned at home from their parents, or from a slave if

Spanish, Italian, and French all have their beginnings in Latin.

they had one. In the richer families, a slave called a *pedagogus* walked boys and girls to the *ludus*, or elementary school.

Class met from early morning until around noon. The teacher (called a *magister*) taught reading, writing, and basic arithmetic. Children wrote with a *stylus* (a pointed tool) on boards covered with beeswax. When they were finished, they smoothed the soft wax over and wrote again. They counted with an abacus, or bead board. Teachers were sometimes very strict.

Most girls left school by age 12. Their mothers then prepared them for marriage and running a home. Boys went on to the *grammaticus*, or high school. They studied public speaking, history, and Greek. They also learned music, geometry, geography, and of course Latin, the Roman language.

Do you speak Spanish, Italian, or French? These languages have their beginnings in Latin. Latin also influenced English. Words like *gloria, templum, difficilis,* and *reparare* all sound like words we use—"glory," "temple," "difficult," and "repair." The Roman alphabet also looked a lot like our capital letters. But their numbers were very different.

Girls left school at the age of 12. Maybe they were glad to get away from the boys' music!

Two plus two is...IV?

Romans wrote their numbers in a system completely different from ours. We use the numerals 1 to 10, but the Romans used seven letters as numerals:

I = 1   C = 100
V = 5   D = 500
X = 10   M = 1,000
L = 50

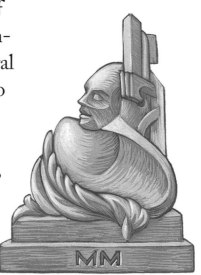

Roman numerals are different from our numbers, but we still use them on objects such as clocks, statues, and buildings. Can you translate the Roman numbers on this page?

Romans wrote their numbers by combining the numerals from left to right, from the largest numeral to the smallest. To read a Roman number like LXVII, you break it down to L (50) plus X (10) plus V (5) plus two Is (1 + 1), for a total of 67.

As you can see, Roman numbers could get long, so the Romans took some short-cuts. Instead of writing a long string of similar numerals (like IIII for the number 4), they would put a smaller numeral in front of a larger one, which meant to subtract it from the larger one. For 4, they would write IV. For 9, it was IX instead of VIIII. 40 is XL, 400 is CD, and 900 is CM. That's why you see statues with dates that start with MCM. That's 1,000 plus 900, or the year 1900.

Confusing? It's a good thing they could erase those wax boards!

A Visit to Rome

Rome was a busy, crowded city 2,000 years ago. It was the heart of the Roman Empire, which stretched across Europe and into Asia and Africa. Imagine what it was like to walk around the great capital city.

As you strolled the streets, you would find them crowded with men. Most women stayed at home, taking care of their houses and families. The men walked everywhere, because the government banned wheel-driven vehicles from sunrise until late afternoon.

But if you were wealthy, your slaves would carry you high above the crowds on a covered litter.

It was always noisy in the city. Workers and shop-keepers cranked open the heavy shutters that protected their workshops and stores, then carried benches and tables loaded with goods to the open sidewalk. Soldiers in leather or chain-mail armor strode past workmen laying water pipes or constructing a new apartment building. Teachers and students recited lessons in little side rooms, shouting over the sounds of goldbeaters, carpenters, boilermakers, barbers, moneychangers, and furniture craftsmen. Street vendors carried sausages and puddings on trays balanced on their heads, and yelled up to women leaning against the open windowsills of their apartments.

Hist-O-Bit

In the early days, Romans wore *togas,* a kind of long sheet they wrapped around themselves. Later, they wore tunics, which looked like a long T-shirt.

Maybe you would go to the Roman Forum, the business and political center of the city. Great speakers debated for hours at the Forum's *comitium*, an open space that was the heart of political life. You could listen for a few minutes, then wander over to watch people do their banking or trading. Businessmen made deals, bankers discussed loans, and moneychangers jingled coins in their hands to attract customers. Other people left offerings at temples dedicated to one of the many Roman gods.

Nearby, in the offices of the Roman Empire, senators and government officials argued over affairs of state. Through the open windows of the courts, you could hear lawyers loudly arguing their clients' cases, along with the shouts and laughter of spectators.

Outside, an argument sometimes became a noisy street fight. Priests and temple musicians led long

Chariot racing was among the most popular sports in ancient Rome. The racers were often formed into teams, and people cheered for their favorite teams and bet on the winners.

funeral processions through the crowds. You would have to be careful—thieves were always watching for a chance to steal from those who weren't paying attention.

In the evening, you would probably go to one of the large open-air theaters, the Colosseum or the Circus Maximus. The performances were free, so poor people enjoyed the same entertainment as did the wealthy—but the rich got better seats.

Back at home, you might light an oil lamp if you were wealthy. Poor people went to bed at dark, since oil was expensive.

As a visitor to the great city, you would find new sights, sounds, and smells around every corner. Rome was loud, dirty, and sometimes dangerous—but no one cared. After all, Rome was the heart of the greatest empire in the world. How could anything be more exciting than that?

Hist-O-Bit

The Circus Maximus wasn't a circus, but an enormous arena where chariot races were held. It was the first and largest arena in Rome.

The Greatest Show in Rome

Rome is even busier than usual. Excited people fill the narrow streets. The emperor is hosting free games at the new arena he has built for the Roman people.

It's called the Flavian Amphitheater, later known as the Colosseum. You can still see its ruins in Rome today. The Colosseum is a huge structure that can seat 50,000 people. Though the games are free, everybody needs an entrance token, made from either clay or bone.

All the staircases and seats are made of marble. There are four levels of seating. Closest to the arena are the senators, nobles, and priests. Only men sit on the first and second levels. The third level is for women only. Their seats are behind a high wall, so the other spectators can't see them. Above them, on the fourth level, are the poor, the slaves, and foreigners.

Suddenly, everybody begins to applaud. The emperor and his friends have entered a magnificent special box beside the arena. Trumpets blare and the

The Colosseum was originally known as the Flavian Amphitheater after the emperors who built it. Their family name was Flavius. The image here is a model.

emperor signals for the games to begin. The gladiators (from the word *gladus,* or "sword") march into the arena and bow to the emperor. They shout, "Hail Caesar! We who are about to die salute you!"

Gladiators are specially trained to fight in the arena. Usually they are slaves, prisoners of war, or convicted criminals. They train for years in gladiator schools, where they specialize in different ways to fight. You can identify each type of gladiator by his weapons. There is a *thracian,* armed with a round shield and a curved sword. A *retiarius* carries a net and trident. Behind them are the *essedarii,* who fight from a chariot. The *bestiarii* are men who fight wild animals.

Gladiators fought each other, as well as wild animals that sprang out of trap doors to surprise them. The battles were usually to the death.

To make the battles interesting, different types of gladiators fight against each other. Some gladiators are quite famous, and the spectators cheer and throw flowers when they see their favorite.

Underneath the arena, a maze of corridors seethes with activity. While the gladiators fight, exotic wild animals such as bears, lions, elephants, and even alligators are hauled up for the next event. Slaves carry away the wounded or dead bodies.

Fights last until one gladiator is defeated. He lifts his left hand, asking the emperor for mercy. Sometimes the emperor lets the spectators decide whether a defeated gladiator will live or die. How would you decide?

Glossary

Abacus A device with beads strung on wires, used to do arithmetic.

Amphitheater A large round arena with seating for many people to watch public events.

Aqueducts Massive irrigation channels that brought water from rivers and lakes to Roman cities.

Archaeologists People who uncover and explain ancient places.

Atrium An open space or courtyard in a Roman home or public building.

Bulla A small pouch or locket that held good-luck charms.

Caesar The emperor of Rome.

Cena The last meal of the day, dinner.

Circus Maximus Arena where chariot races were held, the largest in Rome.

Colosseum The largest amphitheater in Rome, which provided free, violent entertainment.

Comitium An open area used for political activity in the Forum.

Domus Latin for "house."

Dormice Baked stuffed rodents, a delicacy in ancient Rome.

Emperor Ruler of an empire.

Forica Public restroom.

Forum The business, political, and religious center of ancient Rome.

Gladiator A professional fighter who battled, often to the death, for public entertainment.

Grammaticus Roman high school.

Gymnasium Exercise room.

Jentaculum The first meal of the day.

Latrunculi A Roman board game similar to our checkers or chess.

Libra Roman pound.

Ludus Roman elementary school.

Magister Reading, writing, and arithmetic teacher.

Mille passus Roman mile.

Pavimentum The top layer of a Roman road.

Ped Roman foot.

Pedagogus A slave who walked boys and girls to school.

Prandium The midday meal for Romans.

Senator A member of the senate, a council that took part in Roman government.

Stylus A pointed tool used for writing.

Terra-cotta Rough ceramics, from the Latin words for "baked earth."

Thermae Public baths run by the Roman government.

Uncia Roman inch.

Unctorium Room at the public baths where bathers were rubbed with olive oil.

Via Sacra The main street of ancient central Rome.

Villa A country home, usually surrounded by a garden or farmland.

Index

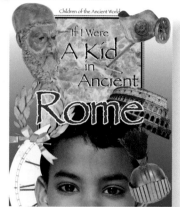

If I Were A Kid in the Ancient World...

What games would I play?
Would I have a pet?
Would I go to school?

Just like kids today, kids of the ancient world played with friends, had pets, went to school, and learned life lessons from their parents. In fact, many of the things kids use and experience today resemble those from ancient times.

Each book in the Children of the Ancient World series looks at what life was like for kids in the ancient regions of Egypt, Greece, Rome, and China. Comparing and contrasting life of kids now as to then, this series presents solidly researched information in a clear, exciting manner that will inspire and attract young readers. Each book is perfect for research or pursuing an emerging interest in the life of ancient times.

Titles in the Children of the Ancient World series

If I Were a Kid in Ancient Greece	APP67929
If I Were a Kid in Ancient Rome	APP67930
If I Were a Kid in Ancient Egypt	APP67932
If I Were a Kid in Ancient China	APP67931

$17.95 each
Order Code: SA20

Cricket Books
www.cricketmag.com
800-821-0115

Our books are available through all major wholesalers as well as directly from us.